SO-AIV-275

HAVE FUN READING THIS BOOK!

IT OFFERS SOME REAL SURVIVAL TIPS. BUT THE SETTINGS ARE NOT REAL. THINK ABOUT HOW YOU CAN USE THESE HACKS IN REAL LIFE. USE COMMON SENSE. BE SAFE AND ASK AN ADULT FOR PERMISSION AND HELP WHEN NEEDED.

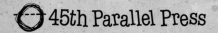
45th Parallel Press

Published in the United States of America by Cherry Lake Publishing
Ann Arbor, Michigan
www.cherrylakepublishing.com

Reading Adviser: Marla Conn, MS, Ed., Literacy specialist, Read-Ability, Inc.
Book Designer: Felicia Macheske

Photo Credits: © Bakai/Shutterstock.com, cover; © GoneWithTheWind/Shutterstock.com, 5; © Dmitrii Iarusov/
Shutterstock.com, 6; © Anna Berdnik/Shutterstock.com, 9; © Thomas Bethge/Shutterstock.com, 11; ©
GoodMood Photo/Shutterstock.com, 13; © Fotos593/Shutterstock.com, 14; © worker/Shutterstock.com,17;
© Yellow Cat/Shutterstock.com, 19; © linyoklin/Shutterstock.com, 21; © sattahipbeach/Shutterstock.com, 22;
© travis manley/Shutterstock.com, 25; © bogdan ionescu/Shutterstock.com, 29

Other Images Throughout:© SrsPvl Witch/Shutterstock.com; © Igor Vitkovskiy/Shutterstock.com; © FabrikaSimf/
Shutterstock.com; © bulbspark/Shutterstock.com; © donatas1205/Shutterstock.com; © NinaM/Shutterstock.com;
© Picsfive/Shutterstock.com; © prapann/Shutterstock.com; © S_Kuzmin/Shutterstock.com © autsawin uttisin/
Shutterstock.com; © xpixel/Shutterstock.com; © OoddySmile/Shutterstock.com; © ilikestudio/Shutterstock.com;
© Kues/Shutterstock.com; © antishock/Shutterstock.com; © Zelimir Zarkovic/Shutterstock.com; © LighteniR/
Shutterstock.com

Copyright © 2020 by Cherry Lake Publishing
All rights reserved. No part of this book may be reproduced or utilized in any
form or by any means without written permission from the publisher.

45th Parallel Press is an imprint of Cherry Lake Publishing.

Library of Congress Cataloging-in-Publication Data

Names: Loh-Hagan, Virginia, author.
Title: Nuclear explosion hacks / Virginia Loh-Hagan.
Description: Ann Arbor, MI : Cherry Lake Publishing, [2019] | Series: Could
 you survive? | Includes bibliographical
 references and index.
Identifiers: LCCN 2019006167| ISBN 9781534147850 (hardcover) | ISBN
 9781534150713 (pbk.) | ISBN 9781534149281 (pdf) | ISBN 9781534152144
 (hosted ebook)
Subjects: LCSH: Radioactive fallout survival—Juvenile literature. | Nuclear
 explosions—Environmental aspects—Juvenile literature. |
 Survival—Juvenile literature.
Classification: LCC TD196.R3 L64 2019 | DDC 363.738—dc23
LC record available at https://lccn.loc.gov/2019006167

Cherry Lake Publishing would like to acknowledge the work of The Partnership for 21st Century Skills.
Please visit *www.p21.org* for more information.

Printed in the United States of America
Corporate Graphics

Dr. Virginia Loh-Hagan is an author, university professor, former classroom teacher, and curriculum designer.
She wants to build an underground bunker. She lives in San Diego with her very tall husband and very naughty
dogs. To learn more about her, visit www.virginialoh.com.

COULD YOU SURVIVE

A NUCLEAR EXPLOSION?

THIS BOOK COULD SAVE YOUR LIFE!

A **nuclear explosion** is a quick release of energy. It's dangerous. It happens when an **atom** is split. Atoms are the basic units of an element.

Nuclear explosions make big blasts. They create lots of heat. They cause damage. They can kill living things. They create **radiation**. They make things **radioactive**. They give off radiant energy. This energy is poisonous.

Time is important in a nuclear explosion. First, the nuclear bomb goes off. This spreads poison in the air. It creates a big mushroom cloud.

Second, radioactive dust and ash fall from the sky. This is called **fallout**. It may look like a hard, black rain. Oil globs may fall like rain. This stuff is dangerous. It can travel for hundreds of miles. It travels in the wind. It **pollutes** the air. Pollutes mean to make dirty or dangerous.

Radioactivity decreases over time. After 7 hours, fallout loses 90 percent of its power. After 2 days, it loses 99 percent. After 2 weeks, only 0.1 percent of radiation will remain. However, even that tiny amount can still be deadly.

Nuclear explosions can make people sick. They blind people. They can cause death. In comic books and movies, they can also create **mutants**. Mutants are deformed. They're monsters. Some may have superpowers.

TIP Move fast. You have 10 to 15 minutes to get away from an explosion.

But, you might be one of the lucky survivors. You have to be smart. You have to stay calm. First, don't touch anything! Keep away from anything that radiates. Second, get away from the radiation area. Get to safety. Most importantly, know how to survive. Keep this in mind:

- You can only live 3 minutes without air.

- You can only live 3 days without water.

- You can only live 3 weeks without food.

This book offers you survival **hacks**, or tricks. Always be prepared. Good luck to you.

TIP Leave the area by moving perpendicular to the path of the fallout. Perpendicular means at a right angle.

SCIENCE CONNECTION

The nucleus is the central part of atoms. Fission is the process of splitting atoms. The nucleus is what gets broken up. Nuclear fission can happen by itself. This is called radioactive decay. Humans can also create nuclear fission. That process is called a nuclear reaction. Nuclear power plants make nuclear energy. About 20 percent of America's electricity comes from nuclear energy. Nuclear energy is a clean energy source. This is because it doesn't burn fuel. It doesn't leak bad gases in the air. Nuclear energy comes from the splitting of uranium atoms. Uranium is a radioactive metal. Its nucleus is unstable. It's always looking for a more stable arrangement. Nuclear power plants split uranium. This fission makes heat. The heat makes steam. The steam runs a machine that makes electricity. Water is used to cool the uranium. Otherwise, the uranium could overheat and melt.

CHAPTER 1

MAKE THICK WALLS!

Oh no! There was a nuclear explosion. Get as far away as you can. Build a safe shelter. Make your own **concrete**. Concrete is a thick building material. It can keep out radiation.

TIP Find an underground shelter.

HACK

1. Get mud from around a body of water. Or make mud. Mix soil and water. Make sure the mud has clay in it.

2. Get **straw**. Straw is dry or dead grass. Mix it with mud and water.

3. Pour the mud mixture on a **tarp**. Tarps are plastic sheets. Put more straw on top.

4. Stomp on the mud and straw.

5. Roll the mud and straw out. Make a flat layer.

6. Fold it onto itself. Add more straw. Stomp again.

7. Shape the mud and straw. Form into bricks.

8. Let the bricks dry.

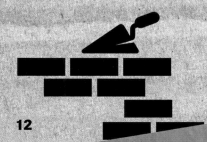

explained by
STEM

The key to this hack is the cob.

Cob is a natural building material. It's made of soil, water, and straw. It's been used since ancient times. Mud is sticky dirt. Straw binds everything together as one piece. Its **fibers** are strong. Fibers are like little threads. Straw makes the shelter strong. It stops the shelter from cracking. It stays together in earthquakes. Explosions can cause the earth to shake.

Explosions also cause fires. Cob houses are **fireproof**. They keep fires out. They have excellent **thermal mass**. Thermal mass is the ability to take in and store heat. Cob houses absorb sunlight during the day. They warm the building.

TIP Wear warm clothes. It gets really cold after an explosion.

CHAPTER 2

FILTER THE AIR!

Nuclear explosions poison the air. Cover your face. Cover your skin. If you have to go outside, wear an air **filter**. Filters let things pass through. They also keep things out. Make your own filter.

TIP Close all vents. Close and seal doors and windows.

HACK

1. Get an empty water bottle. Cut holes in the middle.

2. Get some T-shirts. Fold and roll them up. Wrap them around the bottle.

3. Use strings. Tie the top and bottom. Seal any gaps.

4. Suck air from the water bottle.

5. Breathe in with your mouth. Breathe out with your nose.

TIP Don't collect rainwater. The rain could have poison.

explained by
STEM

The key to this hack is the water bottle.

Water bottles are containers. They hold **liquids**. Liquids are water forms. When not holding water, they hold air. Empty water bottles are full of air. Air takes up space.

Bad air comes in through the water bottle. But it has to pass through the shirts. The shirts are made of cloth. Cloth is made of tiny fibers. It acts as a filter. Most **particles** will be trapped in the cloth. Particles are tiny bits. Cloth keeps bad air out. It keeps the good air in the bottle.

REAL-LIFE CONNECTION

On April 26, 1986, the Chernobyl nuclear power plant exploded. Fire burned in this area of Russia for 9 days. Over 56 people died. Over 4,000 people got sick. Over 50,000 people left the area. They left their dogs. Their dogs were exposed to radiation. The dogs became wild. They have short lives. Today, hundreds of stray dogs still live in the area. They're the kids and grandkids of the original dogs. They have hard lives. They live in freezing weather. They get attacked by wild animals. A group is trying to get the Chernobyl puppies adopted in the United States. The dogs get cleaned up. Radioactive dust is removed from their fur. A scientist said, "All the dogs have been screened and examined for any sort of contamination in their bodies. They certainly pose no significant threat to anybody handling them."

CHAPTER 3

CLEAN THE WATER!

Don't eat or drink anything in the radiation area. Filter your water.

TIP Look for running water.

HACK

1. Get a large soda bottle. Cut out the bottom. Keep the cap on. Put holes in the cap.

2. Turn bottle upside down.

3. First, add a layer of large rocks. Then add a layer of small rocks. Then add a layer of sand.

4. Get **hardwood charcoal**. Examples are burned maple or oak. Add a layer of the charcoal.

5. Add another layer of sand.

6. Add a layer of grass or cloth.

7. Hold the bottle over another container. Pour water into the bottle. Let the water filter through.

8. Repeat pouring the water through. Make the water as clean as you can.

STEM

The key to this hack is the design.

The water sifts through the layers. Each layer filters out bad stuff. The small rocks and sand block out dirty particles. They only let clean water pass through. The different sizes of rocks are important. They create space for air. This lets water move through.

The hardwood charcoal leaves good salts and minerals. It also adds healthy things to the water. It absorbs **toxins**. Toxins are poisons. The hardwood charcoal also absorbs **odors**. Odors are smells. If you burn your own charcoal, make sure it's cooled. Clean off the ash.

TIP Find a radio.
Keep up with the news.

CHAPTER 4

WASH IT AWAY!

Clean your entire body. Clean your clothes. Clean off anything radioactive. Remove fallout from everything. Make your own laundry machine.

TIP Blow your nose. Wipe your eyes. Wipe your ears.

HACK

1. Get a large plastic bucket with a lid.

2. Make a hole in the center of the lid.

3. Get an unused toilet plunger. Cut 6 holes in the side of the plunger.

4. Add hot water to the bucket. Fill it halfway.

5. Add laundry soap.

6. Put in the dirty clothes.

7. Put the handle of the plunger through the hole in the lid.

8. Put the lid over the bucket.

9. Plunge up and down.

10. Rinse out, removing soapy water with regular water.

11. Dry the clothes in the sun.

STEM

The key to this hack is the plunger.

The plunger acts as the **agitator**. Agitators are tools. They put something in motion by shaking or stirring. Washing machine agitators move back and forth.

Washing machines slosh clothes in soap. They do this for a while. They spin fast. They spin in a wheel with holes. The wheel is called a **drum**. The holes let water in and out.

Your hack doesn't have a moving drum. So, you need a paddle to move the water. That paddle is the plunger. As the agitator, the plunger turns the clothes around.

SPOTLIGHT BIOGRAPHY

Mareena Robinson Snowden graduated from the Massachusetts Institute of Technology (MIT). She graduated in 2017. She earned a doctorate in nuclear engineering. Doctorates are the highest degrees in education. Snowden was the first African American to do so. She was 30 years old. She studied at MIT for 11 years. She needed time to adjust to MIT. She was often the only African American person in her classes. She joined African American student groups. She hung up pictures of role models. She said, "I had a picture of Katherine Johnson … who was a mathematician and a black woman killing it." Johnson worked at NASA. She helped send people to space. Snowden is special. Only about 2 percent of African Americans study physics. Snowden said she had a lot of support. She learned from both her good and bad experiences. She said, "MIT really tested how strong I am. To be able to demonstrate that strength to yourself—that's the biggest gift."

CHAPTER 5

LET THERE BE LIGHT!

Nuclear explosions cause a lot of smoke. The smoke is dark. It hides the sun. Nuclear fires inject **soot** into the air. Soot is ash. The fires block out the sun. The sun can't reach the earth. A nuclear winter will take place. This will make the world cold and dark. Make your own light.

HACK

1. Get crayons. Bundle several crayons together.

2. Get a T-shirt. Cut off a strip.

3. Put the strip in the middle of the crayon bundle.

4. Get 2 paper clips. Straighten them out. Wrap them around the ends of the bundle. Secure the bundle.

5. Light the strip.

TIP Don't look at the explosion. This could blind you.

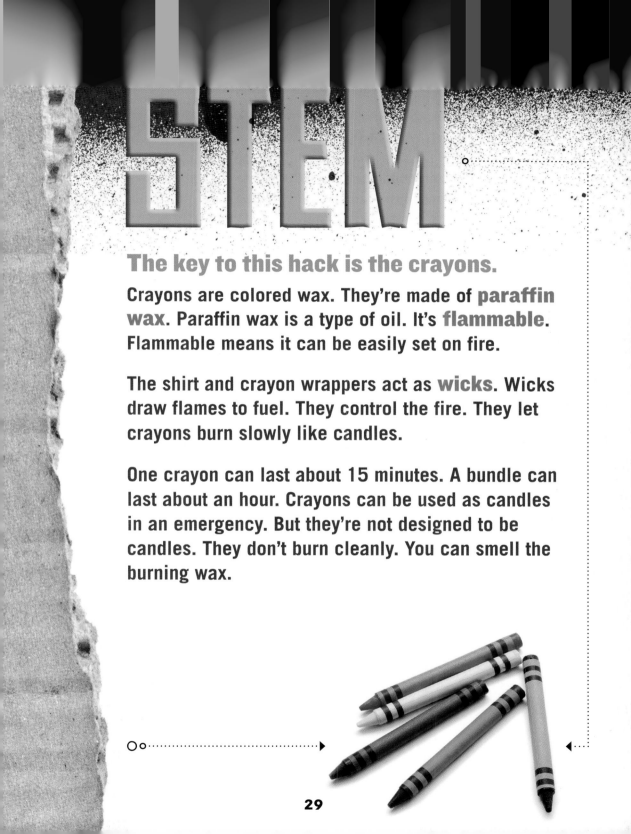

STEM

The key to this hack is the crayons.

Crayons are colored wax. They're made of **paraffin wax**. Paraffin wax is a type of oil. It's **flammable**. Flammable means it can be easily set on fire.

The shirt and crayon wrappers act as **wicks**. Wicks draw flames to fuel. They control the fire. They let crayons burn slowly like candles.

One crayon can last about 15 minutes. A bundle can last about an hour. Crayons can be used as candles in an emergency. But they're not designed to be candles. They don't burn cleanly. You can smell the burning wax.

DID YOU KNOW?

- The first nuclear explosion was a test. It happened on July 16, 1945. It happened on the Trinity Site in New Mexico. It was at the White Sands Missile Range. It's far away from cities and people. It has a lot of wide-open space. The explosion could be seen 180 miles (290 kilometers) away. The unnatural heat changed the sand. It became like glass. It's called trinite. It's illegal to get trinite. Plus, it's still radioactive.

- Nuclear explosions can be used for peaceful reasons as well. They can blow up rocks. They can make big holes. This is useful for mining. It's useful for making canals. It's useful for making harbors.

- Scientists tried to use nuclear power to go to outer space. They worked on Project Orion. They wanted to build a spaceship powered by nuclear bombs. The spaceship would have been big enough for a city full of people. One trip would have used 1,000 nuclear bombs.

- On August 5, 1963, the Limited Test Ban Treaty was signed. Treaty means agreement. The United States, Russia, and Great Britain signed it. They banned the testing of nuclear weapons in space, underwater, and in the air. They could still do testing underground. This treaty was an important step toward controlling nuclear weapons.

- Three Mile Island is in Pennsylvania. A nuclear power plant was there. In 1979, it broke down. It exploded. It released dangerous radiation. It exposed 2 million people. It took 14 years to clean up. It cost $1 billion to clean up. This event led to anti-nuclear movements.

- Russia's Tsar Bomba was the most powerful nuclear weapon ever made. Tsar means ruler. Tsar Bomba was tested in 1961. It made the most powerful man-made explosion in history. Its mushroom cloud was 40 miles (64 km) high. It could be seen 620 miles (998 km) away.

CONSIDER THIS!

TAKE A POSITION!

Learn more about nuclear power. How is it good? How is it bad? Do you think we should use nuclear energy? Argue your point with reasons and evidence.

SAY WHAT?

Learn more about nuclear explosions. Learn about some nuclear explosions in history. Explain the causes of nuclear explosions. Explain the effects of nuclear explosions.

THINK ABOUT IT!

What are some examples of nuclear explosions in comic books? What about movies? What kind of mutant superpowers do characters get? What kind of superpower would you like?

LEARN MORE!

Bell, Samantha. *How Can We Reduce Nuclear Pollution?*. Minneapolis, MN: Lerner Publications, 2016.

Benoit, Peter. *Nuclear Meltdowns*. New York, NY: Children's Press 2012.

Burgan, Michael. *Chernobyl Explosion: How a Deadly Nuclear Accident Frightened the World*. North Mankato, MN: Compass Point Books, 2018.

GLOSSARY

agitator (AJ-ih-tay-tur) a device used to put something in motion by shaking or stirring

atom (AT-uhm) the basic unit of an element

cob (KAHB) a mixture of soil, water, and straw used as building material

concrete (KAHN-kreet) a thick building material made of cement

drum (DRUHM) a moving wheel in a washing machine

fallout (FAWL-out) radioactive dust and ash that fall from the sky after a nuclear explosion

fibers (FYE-burz) small threads

filter (FIL-tur) material that lets things pass through while keeping other things out

fireproof (FIRE-proof) not able to be set on fire

flammable (FLAM-uh-buhl) having the ability to be easily set on fire

hacks (HAKS) tricks

hardwood charcoal (HAHRD-wood CHAR-kohl) burned hardwood like maple or oak

liquids (LIK-widz) water forms

mutants (MYOO-tuhnts) deformed beings or monsters as a result of a nuclear explosion

nuclear explosion (NOO-klee-ur ik-SPLOH-zhuhn) a dangerous explosion caused by the splitting of uranium atoms

odors (OH-durz) smells

paraffin wax (PAR-uh-fin WAKS) wax made from a type of oil

particles (PAHR-tih-kuhlz) tiny bits

pollutes (puh-LOOTS) to poison, to make dirty

radiation (ray-dee-AY-shuhn) the giving off of radiant energy

radioactive (ray-dee-oh-AK-tiv) having dangerous radiant energy

soot (SUT) ash

straw (STRAW) dead or dry grass

tarp (TAHRP) plastic, waterproof sheet

thermal mass (THUR-muhl MAS) the ability to take in and store heat

toxins (TAHK-sinz) poisons

wicks (WIKS) fibers used to draw flames to fuel to make fire

INDEX